G000131158

KEN WORPOLE is a writer and social historian specializing in architecture, planning, urban design and public policy. Whilst teaching English at Hackney Downs School (1969-73), Worpole played a founding role in the creation of Centerprise, an iconic community centre and 'alternative bookshop' in Dalston. Here he was involved in publishing a series of oral histories and radical teaching materials, and reclaiming a number of forgotten working-class writers of East London. This led to the publication of *Dockers and Detectives* in 1984 (new edition 2008), his first significant study. Since then he has released such works as *Towns for People*, *Last Landscapes*, *Modern Hospice Design* and *Contemporary Library Architecture*, as well as a number of collaborative works with photographer Jason Orton, including *350 Miles: An Essex Journey* and *The New English Landscape*. Worpole has served on the UK Government's Urban Green Spaces Task Force, and as an adviser to the Commission for Architecture and the Built Environment. In recent years he has become interested in the ways in which buildings and landscapes still retain the power to offer hope and revelation, and believes that the spirit of political and religious nonconformism still walks abroad, often in the most unexpected places.

NEW JERUSALEM: THE GOOD CITY AND THE GOOD SOCIETY is the fourth in a series of Swedenborg Archive pocket books. The aim of the series is to make available, in printed form, lectures, interviews and other unique items from the Swedenborg Archive that would otherwise remain unseen by a broader audience.

Other titles in the series

1. IAIN SINCLAIR
Blake's London: The Topographic Sublime

2. IAIN SINCLAIR
Swimming to Heaven: The Lost Rivers of London

3. HOMERO ARIDJIS
An Angel Speaks: Selected poems
(Introduction by J M G Le Clezio)

New Jerusalem:
the good city and the good society

New Jerusalem:
the good city and the good society

KEN WORPOLE

The Swedenborg Society
20-21 Bloomsbury Way
London
WC1A 2TH

2017

Typeset at Swedenborg House.
Printed at T J International, Padstow.
Cover and book design © Stephen McNeilly

Published by:
The Swedenborg Society
Swedenborg House
20-21 Bloomsbury Way
London WC1A 2TH

ISBN: 978-0-85448-204-7
British Library Cataloguing-in-Publication Data.
A catalogue record for this book
is available from the British Library.

Contents

NEW JERUSALEM: THE GOOD CITY AND
  THE GOOD SOCIETY...1
Bibliography..71
Acknowledgements..81

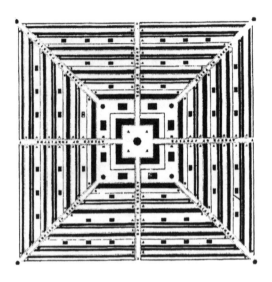

Frontispiece and ornament: Diagram plan for a model city by James Silk Buckingham, 1849.

New Jerusalem:
the good city and the good society

For Joe & Ruby
at home in both the country and the city

I

Begin the world over again: the rise of the garden city movement and early twentieth-century town planning

On 3 December 1898, at Rectory Road Congregational Church in Stoke Newington, London, Ebenezer Howard (1850-1928) gave his first public lecture following the publication of *To-Morrow: A Peaceful Path to Real Reform* six weeks earlier. Republished in 1902 as *Garden Cities of To-Morrow*, this was soon to become one of the most influential town planning documents of the twentieth century. The book was a clarion call for a new world order, replacing the urban slums with garden cities.

Howard was an enthusiastic member of a much

larger late-Victorian network of intellectuals and campaigners calling for social reform during this politically and intellectually tumultuous period. A mild-mannered man, he nevertheless mixed with individuals and organizations wide ranging in their 'progressive' beliefs and affiliations, varying from muscular Christianity to revolutionary socialism, from spiritualism to dress and dietary reform, from women's property rights to the cause of antivivisection, and from Darwinism to 'back to the land' agrarianism. Change was in the air, and universalist in its ambition—nothing less than the creation of a new utopia would do. 'We have it in our power to begin the world over again', Tom Paine had written a century earlier in *Common Sense* (1776), and for Howard and his circle the sentiment still held true.

The pioneering evolutionist Alfred Russel Wallace (1823-1913) was amongst that circle, and, like Howard, was a member of The Brotherhood Church, attending services and lectures at its chapel at the junction of

Southgate Road and Balmes Road in Hackney. This 'ridiculously shabby wooden church', was, according to Maxim Gorky, certainly large enough in 1907 to hold 338 members of the exiled Russian Social Democratic Labour Party, which held its Fifth Congress there, its delegates including Lenin, Trotsky, Stalin and Rosa Luxemburg. The Brotherhood Church was a Christian sect established in the 1880s, with strong socialist and Tolstoyan leanings, and much given to issues of social reform. It had been created by J Bruce Wallace, and a residual membership associated with it is still in existence today—as is the Whiteway Colony in Gloucestershire, a still thriving Tolstoyan community, partly inspired by Bruce Wallace, and founded more than a century ago, in 1898.

In his early days Russel Wallace—no relation to Bruce Wallace—had been a land surveyor and valuer, and was a fervent advocate of land reform; in 1881 he had been active in establishing the Land Nationalisation Society.

Land ownership was a key issue for this and earlier generations of radical reformers, many influenced by the ideas of eighteenth-century radical, Thomas Spence, who maintained that all agricultural land be held and cultivated in common. Howard was firmly persuaded by Spence's ideas, regarding the principle of settlements being built on land owned and managed by autonomous self-governing communities as 'the secular counterparts of the dissenting congregations Howard knew so well', according to biographer Robert Beevers. Public or communal ownership of land, along with development rights and the capturing and redeployment of increases in land values to pay for collective amenities, were to become key principles of the garden city movement, ideas being revived again today.

A further inspiration had been the call for setting up land colonies, made by John Stuart Mill in his *Principles of Political Economy* (1848). Mill commended their efficacy in resolving urban overcrowding by developing new settlements elsewhere—not just in Britain, but as part of the imperial order too. In *On Liberty* (1859) he further argued for 'experiments in living', which he thought desirable to a free society, against the weight of custom thwarting the human capacity for improvement. The nineteenth century saw a proliferation of utopian settlements in Britain—mostly taking the form of agricultural colonies—ranging from the Chartist villages of the 1840s, to a number of Christian messianic communities. These were later joined by similar initiatives undertaken in the names of Ruskin or Tolstoy, as well as anarchist and Fabian socialism, the latter intended principally to bring land and freedom to the urban poor. The utopian spirit— especially in relation to what the Germans called *lebensreform* and what in Britain was designated 'the new life', a combination of personal development through communal living—was alive and well throughout the nineteenth and early twentieth century, and has been well charted by historians such as Gillian Darley, Dennis Hardy and Colin Ward.

Swedenborg and the New Jerusalem
Over time Russel Wallace's role in the development of evolutionary theory——his work is today regarded as important as Darwin's——was overshadowed by his gravitation towards spiritualism and theosophy, in which the ideas of Emanuel Swedenborg played a small but not unimportant part. Trained as a scientist in which he gained international fame, Swedenborg had been an accomplished biologist and pioneer investigator of the human body, and his appreciation of the human form and of Christian conceptions of love, charity and fellow feeling, allowed him to assert that there was a spiritual life as well as a material life, and that the two were connected. The ecstatic affirmation of a spirit world, of something beyond the finitude of earthly life, was convincing to many, even to those committed to practical reform as well. It is Wallace who provides the link between Swedenborgianism,

land reform, and the development of the garden city ideal. *Morning Light*, the weekly newsletter of the New Church, was an early supporter of The Garden City Association (established 1899), and keenly promoted its cause.

The constant recourse to the idea of the utopian city as being the 'New Jerusalem' derived from the Book of Revelation in which a new city of this name is described as descending from heaven to earth and re-establishing another Garden of Eden, and it is the title of one of Swedenborg's most influential works. It was also the inspiration for William Blake's great poem, *Jerusalem* (sung across the political spectrum in Britain, as a hymn to a better world to come), and to historian Tristram Hunt's recent history of Victorian municipalism, *Building Jerusalem*. The 'civic gospel' proclaimed by Joseph Chamberlain was similarly religious in origin, and Hunt is in no doubt that Victorian municipal idealism owed much to Unitarian and other Nonconformist religious beliefs in human betterment. There was a spirit abroad in this period, which combined Christian charity and endeavour, with municipal radicalism and social reform, an animating spirit which resurfaced in the post-war optimism of 1945, which the historian David Kynaston has detailed at length in his trilogy of studies of this period—*Austerity Britain*, *Family Britain* and *Modernity Britain*—and which he collectively chose to call, *Tales of a New Jerusalem*.

Not all utopian visions were rural in outlook, though this was the oldest and most firmly established idyll. In 1884 the Society for Promoting Industrial Villages was established, drawing on the experiences of New Lanark (1786-1825), Saltaire (1850-60), with Port Sunlight (1888) and Bourneville (1893) still to come. In the twentieth century, experimental industrial communities were established at Silver End and the Bata works in Thurrock, both in Essex—and there were others. The harmonious settlement, in which happy workers lived, worked and played, a world away from rural poverty

or urban squalor, was a vision widely shared.
The publication in America in 1888 of Edward
Bellamy's utopian novel, *Looking Backward*,
immediately serialized by The Brotherhood
Church in its journal, suggested that the world's
major cities could also be built anew. Bellamy's
novel swept the world, selling one hundred
thousand copies in two years in Britain alone.

Nevertheless, it is in North America that the
connection between Swedenborgian ideas and
city planning was firmly established. In 1876,
Harvard-educated Swedenborgian minister and
architect Joseph Worcester built his ideal home
at Twin Peaks in the hills of San Francisco,
a shingled bungalow of puritan simplicity,
which quickly became an icon of the early Arts
and Crafts movement in America. Worcester
was well connected, counting the eminent
environmentalist John Muir, landscape architect
Frederick Law Olmsted and writer Jack London
among his friends—the latter writing *Call of the
Wild* whilst staying at Worcester's home in Twin

Peaks. In 1895 Worcester, working alongside architect A Page Brown, commissioned and built the Church of the New Jerusalem close by, a plain wooden building enclosed within a garden, its interior containing an off-centre altar to the east, and a large fireplace to the west flanked by built-in benches. Otherwise there were no fixed pews, just free-standing chairs, with pastoral paintings on the walls, stained glass windows, wooden wainscoting and timber columns supporting the roof left unplaned, displaying the rough bark. The design was widely admired and emulated.

Worcester's influence was also to take much larger dimensions, especially in the work of his young co-religionist and follower, Daniel H Burnham (1846-1912). Burnham's 1909 *Plan of Chicago* was, according to Irving D Fisher, 'deliberately based upon the Heavenly City described in Emanuel Swedenborg's *Heaven and its Wonders and Hell*'. This latter-day exercise in sacred geometry, comprising a monumental network of avenues, buildings,

parks and transport systems, was first explored in
Burnham's designs for the 1893 Chicago World's
Fair, subsequently known as the 'White City', a
model development set in 1000 acres of parkland
designed by Olmsted, and enclosing a grand
artificial lake. The fair attracted over 27 million
visitors, and gave a vision of the world to come.
According to urban historian Helen Meller:

> *The enthusiasm spawned by this vision in
> contemporaries led to the creation of an
> American 'City Beautiful' movement...
> The images of Chicago, both the White City
> and the real one, were to have direct and
> indirect reverberations on the British town
> planning movement well into the twentieth
> century.*

Burnham's monumental designs strongly reprised
the vision of the city described in Bellamy's
Looking Backward, and a new model of urban
living had seemingly arrived and galvanized

city planners across the world. However, what is difficult to understand is how Swedenborg's distinctive preoccupation with the sanctity of the human body as the source of all that is good—an understanding he shared with Blake—was over time reinterpreted as an exercise in system building, no matter how grand and illustrious. Very soon the twentieth century was to become the age of mass democracy, and urban politicians, along with planners and architects, were determined to build towns and cities beautiful to each and everyone. What could go wrong?

II
The great dispersal

Back in Europe, where many older cities were marked by overcrowding, poverty and social unrest, the dominant motive in the early days of town planning was to encourage people to exchange the squalor of the cities for the fresh horizons of country life, whether in rustic colonies or new cities and towns set in rural landscapes. There was often a ruralist heart to British utopianism well into the twentieth century, strongly inspired and shaped by William Morris's utopian novel, *News from Nowhere*, itself a riposte to Bellamy's overly urbane *Looking Backward*. In a letter to

Louisa Baldwin in 1874, Morris summarized his position thus:

> *but look, suppose people lived in little communities among gardens and green fields, so that you could be in the country in five minutes' walk, and had few wants, almost no furniture for instance, and no servants, and studied the (difficult) arts of enjoying life, and finding out what they really wanted: then I think one might hope civilization had really begun.*

Such 'back to the land' sentiments were widely held, and not just in Britain. In France, the economist Jules Méline published *Le retour à la terre* in 1905, arguing for the destruction of the cities and a return to the rural idyll. In Germany the *Wandervogel* movement sought to re-establish an interest in rural ways of life and culture. Anti-urbanism had a long pedigree in European utopian thought, even amongst people for whom the city ought to have been their natural home. The eminent municipal socialist George Lansbury, deeply embedded in East End politics, articulated this seemingly contradictory spirit succinctly when, as leader of the Labour Party in 1934, he said that 'I just long to see a start made on this job of reclaiming, recreating rural England'. The dream of a bucolic rural homeland—Merrie England—remained powerful.

The late nineteenth-century obsession with sanitation, hygiene, and subsequently with eugenics, also played a part, fuelled by the horrors of widespread and preventable urban diseases such as cholera and TB. Ebenezer Howard was much influenced, as were many other planners and reformers, by the long essay by Dr Benjamin Ward Richardson, published in 1876 and dedicated to the great health reformer, Edwin Chadwick, called *Hygeia: A City of Health*. Over time health reform trumped economic and social concerns in the rebuilding of towns and cities. Papworth Village Settlement, founded in

1917 by the Cambridge pathologists Sir Pendrill
Varrier-Jones and Sir German Sims Woodhead,
a village established around a hospital and a
sanatorium was, interestingly, an early member
of the Garden Cities Association, though in
scale and narrowness of focus it was probably
constitutionally ineligible, no matter how worthy.

Howard was unequivocal on this matter.
Speaking at the 1904 British Sociological
Association conference, he said that:

> *I venture to suggest that while the age in
> which we live in is the age of the great,
> closely-compacted, overcrowded city, there
> are already signs, for those who can read
> them, of a coming change so great and so
> momentous that the twentieth century will
> be known as the period of the great exodus,
> the return to the land, the period when by a
> great and conscious effort a new fabric of
> civilisation shall be reared.*

Thus it was that biology rather than sociology took the lead in shaping planning policy at this time. Helen Meller saw it this way:

The role of the municipal councils in promoting the health and welfare of citizens was then at a turning point in the years up to the First World War. As municipalities became caught up in the town planning movement and the problems of housing, the old ideals of 'social citizenship' began to fade. The ideal of the future was very much the garden suburb.

By social citizenship Meller was referring to the civic gospel already mentioned, enthusiastically preached by Victorian municipal reformers, particularly in the northern towns and cities. The emphasis on public works, universal education and the encouragement of a public appreciation of the arts, culture and the enjoyment of well-managed parks and leisure facilities, was intended to bind people together, as a civic, almost republican, whole.

However, a strong element in the counter-vailing resort to environmentalist determinism was the adamant belief that city life was intrinsically malfunctional and malforming. Nowhere was this anti-urban sentiment enacted more explicitly, and more paradoxically, than in London, according to architectural historian, Andrew Saint:

> [F]*or the whole of its existence* [1889-1965] *the LCC* [London County Council] *itself, irrespective of the party in power, also encouraged and promoted the process of 'decentralization' or 'dispersal'...The LCC's long commitment to dispersal highlights the persistence among all British political parties of the puritan distaste for cities and urban life.*

While the rationale for suburban dispersal was

based principally on land prices and availability, along with the widely held belief in the healthier lives to be enjoyed away from the crowded cities, the issue of protecting the civilian population in an age of aerial warfare—first experienced in London during the First World War—was never far from the minds of those in Government. Growing concerns about the impact of war increasingly influenced planning and the forms of future human settlement. 'It is dispersal rather than concentration that gives security to the civilian population in modern warfare', wrote the radical town planner, Thomas Sharp, in 1940, as the bombs began to fall again on London. Sharp wrote this more in sorrow than anger, for he had been a fierce critic of pre-war dispersal policies, which he regarded as creating single-class kraals, as we shall see.

The New Sobriety, or the pub with no beer
While the early LCC cottage estates on London's periphery had good transport connections to and from the city, as well as ample schools and

churches, there were few shops and often no pubs. Thus housing policy was now closely intertwined with moral improvement. The largest of the new estates, such as Downham, Mottingham, Bellingham and Becontree, Saint concluded, 'set a standard for decent working-class housing in the Greater London area on a scale never achieved before. But as communities they were a nullity—suburban commuting ghettoes without the vitality or companionship of the inner city'. At Letchworth, the first and most famous garden city, there was a pub at the outset—The Skittle Temperance Inn—but, as its name suggests, it did not serve beer. Even after the war new towns, such as Harlow in Essex, were characterized by their lack of pubs and social amenities.

The preoccupation with 'hygienic man' as the subject of housing policy reached its apotheosis in early twentieth-century Germany, where the idea of *Existenzminimum* (subsistence dwelling) housing, with its programmatic slogan of 'hygiene, sport and nature' took form. Other variations on this ideal, under the banner of 'The New Sobriety', came with prescriptive ideas about the need for monastic rooms—and single beds for everyone—in floor plans and finishings owing more to the sanatorium or the clinic than to the traditional artisan cottage or tenement building. In Jacques Tati's 1958 film satire, *Mon Oncle*, guests arrive for lunch at the modernist Villa Arpel only to find no furniture, which, as their hostess explains, was proof enough of its modernity. Not quite what William Morris had in mind when he disavowed the clutter of too much furniture. Puritanism, self-denial and a disdain for urban pleasures and attractions became deeply embedded in the early twentieth-century town planning movement.

At the same time, the ideas of evolutionary biologists such as Julian Huxley were being added into the mix. In his capacity as secretary of the London Zoo (1935-42), Huxley had an apartment there which became a meeting place and salon for biologists, ethnologists and modernist architects and designers. Walter Gropius was a very close friend. Some architects he recruited for practical reasons, to help him, in the words of Peder Anker, ensure that 'the infrastructure and buildings of the London Zoo were embedded with modernist visions for urban design and planning'. The Russian émigré architect, Berthold Lubetkin, arrived in England in 1930, and before completing the much-admired Finsbury Health Centre, designed the Penguin Pool at Regent's Park Zoo, which rapidly became an emblem of Huxley's hybrid vision. Lubetkin's firm also designed the Gorilla House there, and a variety of other zoo structures at Whipsnade and Dudley. Huxley once wrote, presumably in a fit of neo-Darwinian fervour, that he hoped one day there would 'no longer be the lamentable contrast between the accommodation provided for the gorillas at the London Zoo and the human population of our towns'. This may be why some people began to think of town planners as men in white coats on a day out from the laboratory or the primate house.

III

*The map is not the territory,
the plan is not the place*

Bellamy's vision of the ideal city in *Looking Backward* was one of visual symmetry and orthogonal order. Early on in the novel his astonished time traveller, Julian West, is led to the top of the house of his host, Dr Leete, where, standing on a belvedere, he looks down at the city below. The view is one of neatly arranged blocks, boulevards and parks, aligned along a strong axial arrangement, and disappearing uniformly and neatly into the distance. Thus it was the plan, or the view from above, which was seen to be the generator of the new way of life——not the new way of life which generated and shaped the plan.

To a large degree this was the case at Letchworth, where all the principal designer— Raymond Unwin, a devotee of the ideas of William Morris—had to work with from the beginning was the famous circular diagram, with a park at its centre, ringed by public buildings, intersected by six radial boulevards. At the perimeter of the circular plan were to be found light industry, allotments and agriculture. This was not a ground plan in any shape or form, but a functionalist formula. 'The concept of the self-sufficient garden city promoted by Howard in *Garden Cities of Tomorrow* (1898-1902)', wrote Andrew Saint, 'having been entirely diagrammatic, Unwin was in effect asked to endow Letchworth with an image and identity. This raised issues of industrial and civic planning, phasing, and investment on a scale that no British architect had hitherto faced'. Letchworth was to be the boldest experiment ever in the creation of an ideal community, yet the irony was that for this sincere socialist, according to his biographer, Frank Jackson, 'domestic privacy was the main virtue'.

Sensitive to artistic values and individual participation, Unwin refused to acknow- ledge the creative flux and sense of mobility enjoyed by modern city-dwellers. His planning was rooted in an ideal of home and privacy, often creating a sense of isolation or inward turning from metropolitan life. 'We must give the individual a place in which he can live, and meditate, retire from the bustle and noise of life, and live what I call a human life', he said in a talk given in Vienna in 1926.

Hitherto, the growth of villages, towns and cities had been largely incremental, producing distinctive local cultures and ways of life—and even temperament. Geography was destiny. However, when faced with a tabula rasa—

whether in the form of a blank sheet of sketch paper or a greenfield site——the temptation to play God proved irresistible.

In her essay, '"The Synoptic View": Aerial Photographs and Twentieth-Century Planning', historian Tanis Hinchcliffe addresses precisely this issue. As contextual history for the rise of the view from the aeroplane on planners, Hinchcliffe summarizes earlier versions of the bird's eye view of the city or the landscape——from hilltop or from balloon——and the dangers 'of designing from the air for people on the ground'. Others saw planners retreating to the nursery, regarding the miniaturization of the scene resulting from an aerial view as a human toy-land, with the architect or planner as the earnest child. Frank Lloyd Wright was not the only architect who ascribed his early interest in architecture to his Montessori-based education, structured around play, using building blocks, shapes and forms.

The eminent planner Patrick Geddes established himself in Edinburgh in his Outlook

Tower, from which he could observe the streets below, a position reprised by film-makers Powell and Pressburger, in *A Matter of Life & Death*, in which a rural doctor is able to study the daily life of his village through the use of a camera obscura. In both of these cases, their view was close enough to the ground to observe the people going about their daily lives, and to learn from these richly variegated patterns of social exchange. This at least had the advantage of an anthropological view. How different, however, was Le Corbusier's interpretation of the city from the air, when, writing of a flight over a city in the 1930s, all he saw so far down below was a spectacle of modular collapse and formal disintegration: too much higgledy-piggledy, uneven heights, back alleys, nooks and crannies. Hinchcliffe concludes that 'the seeds of mass redevelopment of the working-class areas of Paris [such as Belleville and Ménilmontant] reside in the post-war aerial photographs and the type of disapproval they generated'.

The burgeoning slum-clearance and house-building programmes of local authorities in the 1930s led to a proliferation of cottage estates across Britain, planned, designed and built in a spirit of idealism, with ample space, light, greenery and flair. Nevertheless, they tended to be built on cheap, peripheral land and very large in size, their designers, according to Alison Ravetz, 'given to geometric, often concentric, road layouts which made best sense when seen from the air (or on the drawing board) but were labyrinthine and confusing on the ground'. Yet as we saw with regard to the early LCC estates, what they badly lacked was connectivity to the working heart of the city and its many amenities and opportunities.

It was the organizing principle of planning by zoning, separating the housing from the industry, the commercial district from the shopping centres, and the civic from leisure and recreational amenities, which caused so many of the subsequent problems. When ring

roads arrived in many towns and cities in
the 1960s, the housing areas were effectively
cut off from the city centres, physically and
psychologically. The notion of a neighbourhood
or city as a potential or actual 'whole way of
life'—which was the organizing principle of so
many utopian visions—was sundered. Working-
class communities, which had once occupied
the centres of towns and cities (often living,
admittedly, in what were defined as slums),
where people lived and worked in close proximity
to each other, were 'decanted' en masse to newly
built peripheral estates, cut off from familiar
social networks and local economies.

The gains in improved housing over time
were more than offset by the losses in economic
connectivity and social integration. This is the
story told by Beatrix Campbell in *Goliath*, her
account of the disastrous social consequences
of post-war housing policy, as well as being
detailed on the website, *Municipal Dreams*. A
1994 report for the Joseph Rowntree Foundation

into the failure of many inter-war cottage estates
concluded that despite their structural qualities,
'all the back gardens and spacious front rooms
in the world cannot compensate for access to
work and education'.

Not Utopia, but Motopia

The availability of cheap energy proved to be
another malign determinant of urban planning
in the second half of the twentieth century, an
unanticipated but decisive factor. The inexorable
rise of the car and the political power of the
motor industry effectively put a stop to the early
twentieth-century democratic idea of 'planning
for people', or even imagining that urban design
might any longer prioritize social obligations.
Traffic engineering came to dominate local
planning, as had housing policy a generation
before. One of the more bizarre speculations
on a better world to be fashioned came from
landscape architect Geoffrey Jellicoe, in his 1961
futuristic idyll, *Motopia*, developed as a response

to the early realization that 'our present physical conditions are being thrown into chaos by the advent of one car per family and even one per person'. Since then the car has achieved even greater dominance: today there are numerically 2.5 cars for every child in the UK population.

Jellicoe was schooled in two distinct traditions. Firstly, he had been a student of European classical (and geometrical) town planning, with its strong axial lines, wide boulevards and strict hierarchies of scale. Secondly, and somewhat contradictorily, he had also trained as a landscape architect in the picturesque, naturalistic school of English landscape gardening, with its love of informality and unregulated vistas and contours. How to square the circle? The answer was strict separation, in which 'the ideal town would seem to be one in which the traffic circulation were piped like drainage and water; out of sight and mind'.

There was no point in trying to create a utopia by adapting existing cities, Jellicoe insisted, that was merely a case of putting new wine into old bottles. The time had come to create new towns from scratch. The first view of Motopia is once again from above: 'When you come out of the sky upon Motopia, your first view is of a geometric framework of rectangles with circles at the intersection'. Motopia was to be a gridiron of continuous housing blocks, the flat roofs of which form the principal roads. At the intersections of the grid system were roundabouts. Between the housing blocks would be found informal parkland, along with an extensive network of artificial canal and water systems.

In a single glance the principal conceptual idea of Motopia is apparent: 'the separation of mechanical and biological man'. For Jellicoe town planning was a matter of geometry, and the landscape a matter of biology. Significantly, the puritanical impulses lying beneath the surface of this bio-technical version of the modernist movement are evident when Jellicoe chose to describe each apartment as 'the cell'. That noun alone captures a disturbing aspect of the modernist project: the creation of housing settlements where the bio-evolutionary combined with moral improvement, especially for the masses.

The design implications of mass car ownership led to other attempts to develop new settlements, but this time based on the promotion of the residential neighbourhood as a convivial unit. This was the idea of the American Clarence Stein in his famous design for Radburn, New Jersey, founded in 1929 and intended to be 'A Town for the Motor Age'. Although never fully realized, the design was much admired and widely emulated, as it still is today. Like Howard's plans for the first garden city, and Jellicoe's Motopia, Radburn was intended to number 30,000 residents as the ideal size. Stein was happy to admit his plan had originally been inspired by Unwin's layout of Hampstead Garden Suburb.

There were two distinct features to Radburn. The first was the layout of the road system, providing a strong framework at the edges of the estate, but feeding into a subsidiary network of residential cul-de-sacs. There was a completely separate pedestrian network, which children and others could use to walk to school, as well as to the shops and local amenities, without crossing a single road. The absence of through roads effectively reduced local traffic to residents alone, and then only to the streets where they actually lived. From the outset Radburn was designed as a place where the needs of children took priority over provision for cars.

The second innovative feature, borrowed from the garden city model, was that the estate was self-governing, and constitutionally enabled to fund local services and maintenance programmes from levies on residents, who in turn elected the community's governing body. This association had the power to restrict development or changes to properties which were deemed to harm the communal look or ethos of the estate. Such community or homeowners' covenants have not always been benign, of course, and there have been cases where they have been employed to discriminate openly or covertly against new members on grounds of race or religion, though this was not the case at Radburn. In fact the development was widely praised for its diversity of housing sizes and layouts, and the variety of lifestyles and income levels it attracted.

Planning historian Alison Ravetz, described the Radburn cul-de-sac as an attempt to create an 'eye-to-eye democracy'. Similar residential closes became a popular feature of housing developments across the world, as they were deemed to support a sense of neighbourhood or community at an intimate level. Nevertheless, where like-minded developments or layouts were poorly built, or their communal services and spaces underfunded, residents could become isolated from the wider society, and cut adrift—particularly if they didn't have cars. What was originally designed to flourish as a sociable street community could under such conditions become a backwater.

IV

The rise and fall of public housing

Radburn-style layouts were subsequently employed in a number of Britain's post-war 'New Towns', of which 28 were created by 1970, and for which hopes were high, particularly amongst politicians and planners. As with earlier LCC and other municipal estates, design standards and space allowances were good, but there was little or no consultation with would-be inhabitants about what they hoped to see in their new homes and communities, and how these might be arranged. Nor in the case of the new towns was there any detailed consultation with the local authorities

within whose jurisdiction they were located.
The New Towns were directly administered from
Whitehall by Development Corporations, and all
expenditure was controlled by the Exchequer, and
only for approved purposes.

Furthermore, they were rarely designed to
accommodate to the distinctive topography of
their settings, as Alison Ravetz documents:

> *They had no direct relationship with their
> agricultural surroundings, and, far from
> providing self-governing communities, their
> peremptory designation by the Minister
> and the compulsory purchase of their land
> alienated many of the existing, indigenous
> residents. . . local authorities where new
> towns were situated found them a drain on
> their resources for many years, yet had no
> political or financial control over them.*

Even so, public housing programmes proceeded
apace, still largely without any social stigma

attached to the homes or their residents. Aneurin Bevan, famously Labour's post-war Minister for Health was also, simultaneously, Minister for Housing, and for him at least health and housing were then seen as being inextricably linked. It was Bevan who evoked the ideal of housing as part of a 'whole way of life' when he said that:

> *We should try to introduce into our modern villages and towns what was always the lovely feature of English and Welsh villages, where the doctor, the grocer, the butcher and the farm labourer all lived in the same street. I believe that it is essential for the full life of a citizen to see the living tapestry of a mixed community.*

Bevan's dream had been influenced by the 1940 Penguin book, *Town Planning*, by Thomas Sharp already mentioned. Sharp excoriated inter-war experiments in large-scale decanting

as producing 'social concentration camps',
single-class ghettoes, even if the housing was
new, and the design of many of these cottage
estates was visually attractive. 'Around the
great cities', he recorded, 'we have enormous
one-class communities (if they can be called
communities) the like of which the world has
never seen before; Becontree, where no less
than 120,000 working-class people live in one
enormous concentration: Norris Green, one of
many Liverpool Corporation Estates, housing
50,000 working-class inhabitants'.

By the end of the 1970s, nearly half of the
British population lived in council housing
(later relabelled social housing and, even later,
with no hint of irony, affordable housing, as if
affordability suggested a want of aspiration).
Despite the lack of consultation over matters of
design, and the disconnection of too many large
estates from city centre amenities, for several
decades new public housing came to many people
as a godsend, a point firmly reiterated by writer

John Grindrod in his recent trenchant defence, *Concretopia*. And as his fellow former council tenant, Lynsey Hanley, further reminds us, 'the gap between the highest and lowest incomes in the country reached its narrowest in 1979, the same year in which the largest proportion of the population lived in local-authority housing'. That was also the year which elected a new Conservative government under Margaret Thatcher, and inequality began to rise again.

The sale of council houses under the 'Right to Buy' scheme introduced by the 1979 Conservative government, amounted to Britain's biggest privatization of public assets by far, totalling some £40 billion in the first 25 years. The money was not used to build more houses, however, but to underwrite the effects of spending cuts elsewhere in public services. According to James Meek, 'Before Right to Buy, the government spent a pound on building homes for every pound it spent on rent subsidies. Now, for every pound it spends on housing benefit, it puts five pence towards building'.

Many of the homes sold to their owners were then sold on to others, including property companies which subsequently exploited former publicly subsidized assets to their own financial advantage. What had been until then stable local authority estates witnessed an increasing turnover of tenants as newly privatized homes were let and sublet with greater frequency. Continuity of residency (contributing to a degree of community) was replaced by 'churn'. In 1994 there were still nearly five million council homes in Britain, by far the largest stock of publicly owned and run housing in the Western world, according to Anne Power and Rebecca Tunstall. Built with the best of intentions, and often designed to promote neighbourliness and a sense of community, the problem was that now most of it had resulted in 'large, separate, single-class, single use estates'. Public housing had, in the ungainly vocabulary of the twenty-first century, been 'residualized'.

An unintended consequence of what
was ostensibly a political desire to increase
homeownership and extend freedom of choice
(as well as win elections), over time resulted in
its exact opposite. Homeownership in the UK is
now in decline. Compared with other European
countries the UK is now almost at the bottom
of the league table of householders who own
their own property, and has returned to a *rentier*
economy, with millions of people now relying
on housing as a source of finance, according
to Danny Dorling. Today UK rents are amongst
the highest in Europe, and new British homes
amongst the smallest.

There is no doubt at all that many large
public housing estates designed and built in
the twentieth century in Britain were inspired
by political and professional idealism, or
utopianism. The extensive archival website
Municipal Dreams has more than adequately
detailed the scale and ambition of the UK
local authority housing project throughout its

twentieth-century history, which also occurred across Europe, with the right to a decent home being recognized across the political spectrum as a fail-safe of a mature and settled democracy. Largely as a result of 'Right to Buy' and cuts to budgets, as well as powerful ideological pressures to turn Britain into a 'property-owning democracy', by 2008 there were 170 councils in Britain which no longer provided public housing of any kind. They had thus abandoned any responsibility for meeting some of their electorate's most basic needs.

What it's like to live there?

It is the private sector which governments today deem the most appropriate provider of housing in Britain, even in a period in which owner-occupation is in decline, and house buying is beyond the means of many, especially the young, even in full-time employment. In 2005 The Commission for Architecture and the Built Environment (CABE) published a report called

What it's like to live there: the views of residents on the design of new housing, based on interviews with 241 residents from 11 new housing schemes in three northern regions and three in the south-east, designed to assess 'the quality of new private housing getting built in England today'. This in its own way was a test of what kinds of neighbourhood or community were being designed in a post-Radburn, post-New Town era.

The most striking finding was the dominance of the private car on people's perceptions of the desirability of where they lived: residents wanted more car parking spaces for each property, with additional car parking for approved visitors, whilst avoiding the inclusion of any through roads. The cul-de-sac had wreaked its revenge. It was now seen as the most car-friendly form of housing layout, seemingly providing the look and feel of gated communities. Many adult residents interviewed said they used a car for most if not all of their journeys from home, and some admitted never having walked anywhere locally, nor, by implication, explored the surrounding fields and footpaths where they lived, despite some of the new estates being built on greenfield sites.

'In most of the developments there seems to be little or no social interaction between residents', the report noted, further suggesting that, 'aspirational lifestyles seem to be identified with exclusivity and owning more and larger cars rather than sustainable forms of transport and layouts where the pedestrian takes precedence over the car'. In general, home buyers wanted larger houses, more car parking and greater domestic privacy, and appeared uninterested in matters of environmental sustainability—which the architectural and construction industries are now required to address, no matter how superficially. The CABE research concluded rather despairingly that what people said they wanted, and what housing professionals and politicians wanted on their behalf, were currently incompatible. The competing interests of individual choice and buying power, and a need to finance and provide collective amenities, had produced political stalemate.

The dilemma as to how to develop more appropriate forms of settlement is likely to resolve itself as a result of increasing demographic change. The inflexibility of current models of town extensions, executive estates, and dormitory settlements, may be their undoing. The rise of the single-person household——now 28% in the UK (but astonishingly over 40% in Sweden)——includes a large proportion of older people needing access to shops, health and other personal services, and is reconfiguring neighbourhoods (and even whole towns). According to the 2014 Office for National Statistics, Families and Households data, two-person households today make up the largest proportion of UK households (35%), single-person households come next (28%), and households with four or more people, the conventional view of the family home, now constitute only 20% of all households.

Equally pressing are major changes in the labour market, with the rise of live/work lifestyles and economies, with a concomitant increase in self-employment and freelance working. In a new study of working households, architectural historian Frances Holliss, writes that,

> *The spatial separation of dwelling and workplace emerges as a basic and apparently little questioned premise for urban planning and design. Although housing conditions were improved for the poorest of the population, home-based work, a valuable social, economic, architectural and urban practice, was driven under-ground. Men and women today often work at home so that they can combine domestic and breadwinning roles. Cities designed to reflect and accommodate this would take a radically different form.*

Nearly 25% of the UK working population now works at home for at least eight hours a week. Women today make up half the workforce (proportionately higher in some UK cities), another significant dynamic in the shape and feel of modern economic and social life. Meanwhile, some 16% of UK households are workless. The enormous changes in the labour market, as well as in education (where nearly half of young people now attend university), are reshaping the pattern of daily life, but are barely reflected in models of house-building and town planning, where the dormitory suburb still dominates as the ideal type.

The proposal for a new Garden City by David Rudlin and Nick Falk of URBED, which won the 2014 Wolfson Economics Prize, is a bold attempt to address many of these issues, as well as correct some of the weaknesses of Howard's original model. The plan imagines grafting large new areas of development onto an existing city, thus taking advantage of amenities already in

place——schools, libraries, university, general
hospital, retail centre, railway station and related
transport infrastructure. The authors admit
refreshingly that, 'You cannot build a *Garden City*
from scratch'. The controversial element is that
development at this scale can only be achieved
by acquiring green belt land at the price of land
sold without permission to develop. This is much
cheaper of course, but at first sight, contradictory.
However, the argument for doing so is that the
'unearned increment' of rising land values will be
held in trust for communal benefit. The proposal
is closely argued and seemingly financially
viable. What is less clear is that at the level of the
neighbourhood and the street, the regulatory
frameworks (and indeed social covenants)
required to underpin the social dynamics of
mixed use, mixed tenure neighbourhoods——
against the 'creative destruction' of the property
market——are not provided.

V

Elective affinities

P ast templates for the good society were often cast in brick or stone prematurely. Designing for greater self-sufficiency in livelihood and well-being has few historical precedents, and the paucity of social experimentation can be seen by how the same few radical exemplars are cited again and again in twentieth-century British architectural history—The Pioneer Health Centre, Finsbury Health Centre, Silver End, New Ash Green, Byker Wall, Eldonian Village and Bedzed. Yet people have always dreamed of buildings which, in the words of architectural historian Thomas A Markus,

'satisfied the deepest longings for both justice
and the creation of bonds [which would] house
the structure-less, power-less societies envisaged
by both Marxists and Christians in visions
so central to the Western tradition'. Markus's
seminal work, *Buildings and Power*, alludes to
just two formations containing such a utopian
element——the pastoral colony and the perfect
city of production——to some degree echoed in
the nineteenth-century Chartist colonies and the
philanthropic industrial settlements.

According to philosopher Immanuel
Wallerstein: 'Utopias have religious functions
and they can also sometimes be mechanisms
of political mobilisation. But politically they
tend to rebound. For utopias are breeders of
illusions and therefore, inevitably, of disillusions.
And utopias can be used, have been used, as
justifications for terrible wrongs'. Anarchist
thinker and writer Colin Ward, likewise saw all
distant goals as a form of tyranny, and believed
that anarchist principles were better discerned

in everyday human relations and impulses. These were 'the seeds beneath the snow' of daily cooperation and goodwill. The human impulse to do good rather than bad, to tell the truth rather than lie, were sufficient grounds for believing that any attempt to create the conditions for the good society must be rooted in the here and now, 'in the very world, which is the world/Of all of us,—the place where in the end/We find our happiness, or not at all!', as Wordsworth wrote in his more idealistic youth.

Such principles are explored in Tobias Jones's recent book, *Utopian Dreams*, a timely essay on contemporary utopian theory, focusing on modern experiments in living. Jones was inspired to experience communal living because he was 'fascinated simply to find out what it feels like to believe in something, actually to believe that the world could get better rather than worse'. What he discovered was that the deepest need met by the many different communities he encountered was for some larger purpose or meaning in

life, which he surmised the 'sacred canopy' of
religion once offered to all.

Together with his wife and young daughter,
Jones spent several months at a time in a variety
of political, New Age and religious communities
in the UK and Italy, finding much to admire
in all of them, but sooner or later wishing to
leave, if not actually flee. Too often there was a
covert sense either of being one of the elected,
or having to swallow whole a collection of
prescriptions about the good life which brooked
little dissent. The one community which worked
best in his view required no commitment at all to
membership, let alone long-standing residency.
Christian in origin, and based in the West Country
in a large stone rural monastic settlement from
the 1640s, Pilsdon remains open to absolutely
anybody who walks through its door (as long as
they come without alcohol or drugs).

Some residents, the 'regulars', have been there
for a while, whilst others, the 'wayfarers', come and
go at will, sometimes staying for as little as a single

night. Nearly all have led troubled lives, afflicted by mental illness, drug addiction or alcoholism, but the community offers them shelter, companionship, as and when needed, as long as residents help with the daily work of cleaning, cooking and tending the small estate. The crucial lesson Jones learned was that while it has always been assumed that utopian communities can only succeed on the basis of continuity of membership, and intensity of attachment, this may be a grave misconception. If the ethos of the community is strong enough, Jones suggests, and the 'rules of engagement' clearly understood, then members can come and go as needed, so long as there is a nucleus of 'regulars' to keep the settlement open and working.

Returning to Bristol, Jones looked closer to home, realizing that where he already lived was itself the setting of many smaller, communal initiatives. These thrived on the basis of informality and focus: whether to work with drug addicts, to provide shelter for abused women and children, to grow food communally, or to repair and recycle furniture for people in need, along with other objectives. Such projects worked precisely because they lacked overly ambitious aims or indulged in system building. 'I'm feeling less apocalyptic than I was a year or two ago', the author concluded. 'With each passing month I hear about a new gathering of humans, trying to work out the best way to live together. They don't live in secrecy, but nor do they have bell-towers, spires or grandiose sandstone architecture. If you didn't look for them, you wouldn't ever know they were there'.

Though Jones doesn't allude to it, these are Edmund Burke's 'small platoons', leavening the bread of civil society, and despite disavowing the need for a new utopian architecture, it is significant that he is currently managing a woodland experiment in community building, which requires participants to help build and garden for themselves. In the end there is no escape from architecture, no matter how modest or improvised. Behind any social arrangement there is a physical structure, a location and a landscape as well.

Dylan Evans provides another contemporary account of an attempted model community in *The Utopia Experiment*. In 2006 Evans sold his house to fund the setting up of a self-sufficient community in Scotland, welcoming volunteers to join him in preparing for a post-apocalyptic world. Few of the participants had practical skills, though they had many and varied millenarian beliefs. Though not quite a disaster for all of them, it was for Evans, resulting in a serious mental breakdown requiring hospitalization.

In an honest, self-critical account of his project, Evans is interested in finding out why so many attempts to create utopian communities fail. 'I suspect', he writes, 'it may be something to do with the very idea of wiping the slate clean, of resetting the clock to year zero, and building anew from scratch. For while the institutions that the idealists wish to replace are often riddled with flaws, they also embody the accumulated wisdom of many generations'. This again echoes Edmund Burke, who argued that while social institutions take time to establish, they can all too easily be destroyed, too frequently with nothing to put in their place. Be careful what you wish for.

Utopian thought shares some of the impulses of intense religious attachment. Eileen Barker, a leading authority on new religious movements and cults, has suggested that many of these groupings possess both positive and negative features, which students of utopianism will certainly recognize. Most who join such communities eventually leave unharmed, and some are even strengthened by their involvement. However, Barker also notes the danger signals which occur when good intentions go astray. These are, she suggests: a) when a movement cuts itself off geographically or socially from the rest of society; b) its members increasingly rely on other members

for their definition of 'reality'; c) when sharp
distinctions begin to be made between 'them'
and 'us'; d) important decisions about members'
lives are made by others; e) leaders claim special
privileges or divine authority; f) leaders and
movements become obsessed with a single goal
pursued at the cost of all other aspects of life.
Jones and Evans experienced elements of nearly
all of these.

Scepticism about the possibility of building
a better future is widespread today. The former
agencies of social change—religious and social
movements, trades unions, political parties and
municipal reformers—struggle to retain any
leverage on public policy, as globalization erodes
power at national and even international levels,
and corporations come to dominate economic
and political decision making, even down to the
level of the neighbourhood and the street.

One area of new housing offers inspiration,
and that is in the provision of residential
communities for older people, where common

services and facilities are now an integral part
of the design. Today these operate at a scale
from the single residential home to an entire
settlement, such as that at New Earswick in York,
pioneered by the Joseph Rowntree Foundation.
New thinking about housing design for older
people——for those still leading active lives as
well as those with disabilities and chronic health
conditions requiring high levels of personal
care——draws inspiration from monastic and
almshouse traditions, as well as from the
burgeoning therapeutic communities movement
of the twentieth century.

This latter movement, now formalized
through the work of the Planned Environmental
Therapy Trust, developed in response to the
trauma of the First World War, and sought to
bring the insights of Freudian psychology to the
residential provision of traditional asylums and
hospitals. The ideal of the therapeutic community
influenced mainstream mental health provision,
especially in the design of new hospitals for those

with mental health problems requiring both custody and care. My own father was one such patient in the 1950s, at Runwell Hospital in Essex, opened in 1937, but whose origins can be directly traced back to the First World War. The design of Runwell broke with conventional asylum architecture. Instead of a monumental Victorian barracks behind high walls, this former farmland estate was laid out as a series of villas and chalets, each with its own gardens and common dining and washing facilities. Patients were allocated to particular villas or chalets according to their condition, and were encouraged to become part of a small 'family' of fellow patients, eating and socializing with each other, as well as maintaining their own patch of garden.

New urban villages

The rich and varied history of the therapeutic communities movement is still too little appreciated, but in the modern world there are more forms of communal living than many realize——religious, political, environmentally self-sufficient, therapeutic——nearly all of which embody utopian elements, both in their values and design. It is not just older people whose accommodation needs require more imaginative solutions, solutions which not only provide shelter and care, but forms of mutual aid and social engagement, which give life meaning. Contemporary pioneers in housing policy and urban design are now focusing on the need to rebuild neighbourhoods, and provide more adaptable forms of housing in new configurations, which can be designed or retrofitted to accommodate people at all stages in their lives, and in a variety of living arrangements. Frances Holliss, a strong advocate of live/work arrangements, concludes that cities designed to accommodate more flexible patterns of working and living——especially for women, who now make up more than half the workforce in a number of UK cities——would architecturally and socially look and feel very different.

Compared with earlier programmes of mass
housing, it is in the world of work and production
that imaginative initiatives in building design
and adaptation have surfaced. These draw on
economic theories first formulated by Alfred
Marshall in the 1890s, who advanced the idea
that it is in the form of industrial 'clusters' by
which regions, cities and even neighbourhoods
prosper, concentrating on particular trades or
industries, often but not always drawing on
topographical advantage. Thus shipbuilding in
Glasgow and Tyneside, jewellery and toolmaking
in Birmingham, shoemaking in Northampton
and furniture making in Hackney, are among
many examples. Today clustering theory has re-
emerged with a vengeance.

In a post-industrial society, such
concentrations now take the form of silicon
valleys and corridors, tele-villages, fashion
districts, media and artists' quarters, along with
other congeries of related trades and professions
now encouraged to share a roof in managed or

shared workspaces, where individuals and small businesses are able to trade with each other and benefit from common services. What is more, these smaller enterprises depend heavily on face-to-face meetings and networks to succeed, which is why the coffee house has once again become a central feature of many new urban quarters.

In his 1964 essay, 'The Urban Place and the Non-Place Urban Realm', the American urban designer Melvin Webber coined a phrase which anticipated the changing nature of future social relations in the modern world: *community without propinquity*. By this he meant that the communities of the future would increasingly be based on shared interests and identities, rather than physical proximity. In its crudest interpretation this was taken to suggest that the neighbourhood was dead. Presciently, Webber advanced his theory long before the Internet enabled interest-based communities—whose reach now extends across the globe—to become even more commanding.

Despite the general truth of this prediction, there is now a growing desire to reinstate face-to-face relations at the heart of social well-being. In her advocacy of the value of 'the village effect', social psychologist Susan Pinker points to the many benefits which accrue to human beings who enjoy a variety of face-to-face relationships on a daily basis. The 'power of proximity', as she calls it, is not only vital to the well-being of older people, who may well suffer from isolation, but is important to young people too. Pinker realized this when looking at educational failure in working-class or deprived communities where it is possible to drop out of education unnoticed, especially where students have to travel some distance to attend college or school. In her native Quebec it is called *décrochage* (unhooking), and up to 40% of high school students do so. What gets them back on track are not exhortatory emails or standardized letters to the family home, but personal meetings on a regular basis, by sympathetic support staff. Distance learning

programmes and online social networks may work
for some, but the best mentoring and educational
relationships are embedded in face-to-face contact
and understanding, and here neighbourhood
facilities and attachments work best (as they
clearly do in the moral sphere as well).

In today's more diverse neighbourhoods, the
housing equivalent of the managed workspace
or the live/work quarter is slowly developing
in the form of co-housing, well established
elsewhere in Europe. Co-housing takes many
forms, whether as collective self-build initiatives,
as mixed social-rental and owner-occupier
settlements, or as private endeavours, the lease
conditions of which require homeowners to
contribute to, and abide by, an agreed set of
communal amenities and social obligations.
Hedgehog Co-op in Brighton, established in the
1990s, is a self-build community, with firm roots
in the neighbourhood, all of whose original
members are still in place and thriving. Ashley
Vale Action Group bought a disused scaffolding

yard in Bristol in 2000, and members have since designed and built a variety of timber-framed, ecologically sustainable homes (41 to date), along with a community centre and allotments. The Threshold Centre in Dorset consists of 14 dwellings, 7 in shared ownership with a local housing association offering affordable rents, and seven privately owned. It also operates as a sustainable education centre, with a common house and market garden. Cambridge City Council and Cambridge Cohousing are currently collaborating on a scheme to provide 40 energy-efficient homes designed by Mole Architects with developer TOWNhus at Orchard Park, Cambridge, whose residents will have a choice of floor plans, number of rooms, interior and exterior finishes, in a shared landscape, and with a common house for communal activities.

These are just a handful of a growing number of co-housing initiatives which seek to marry the provision of new homes with social, educational and workplace amenities and opportunities——a far cry from the speculative, one-size-fits-all housing estates offered by volume builders. None require members to spend the rest of their lives in one place, but tenants or buyers replacing them are equally required to accept and comply with the ethos and obligations of the founding agreement. Such buildings and settlements provide different sizes of apartments, as well as a range of tenure options and common services—utilities rooms, computer suites, guest apartments, play facilities, communal gardens— thus offering opportunities for a more sociable and creative urbanity than is provided by a proliferation of random and impersonal buy-to-let properties on one-year contracts, the growth of which now contributes to the unravelling of many once cohesive neighbourhoods in London and other cities.

These projects are more in the tradition of the open house rather than the closed community. This would be a significant step towards the creation of genuine 'urban villages', a concept to date which, according to Liz Greenhalgh, 'if scrutinised, in reality [means] housing areas simply given an urban gloss'. In areas of high property demand, economic pressures invariably result in the conversion of most potential workspaces (warehouses, small industrial buildings) into residential flats, eradicating any possible balance between different income groups, or between work, living and social spaces— which is what a successful urban village would require. Community land trusts, covenants and other land-use planning instruments are needed to challenge the tyranny which corporate finance now exerts on urban land values, as demonstrated by the example of Coin Street Community Builders, a social enterprise which created a thriving mixed community on London's South Bank, formerly intended for high-rise luxury apartments.

The word *Utopia* is derived from the Greek compound meaning 'No-where'. It is why Morris's utopian novel was called *News from Nowhere*, and there have been fictional descriptions of many other 'nowheres', before and since, starting with Thomas More. Yet we should also set against this imaginative genre, the admonitory words of novelist, Elizabeth Bowen: 'Nothing can happen nowhere'. Somewhere between the idyll and the reality of daily life, there is a need to create new forms of neighbourhood and community. Many have been inspired by the Granby Four Streets community land trust in Liverpool, working with architecture collective, Assemble, to refurbish four dilapidated but handsome streets, slated for demolition——a project shortlisted for the 2015 Turner Prize. Whether custom-built or adapted, whether managed by development trusts, housing associations, local authorities, co-ownership groups or even private developers, the utopian experiments of the future might better succeed—— not as closed communities——but as settlements and networks in an open city, where the principle of hope is not that of the manifesto or master-plan, but of elective affinities.

Bibliography

Anker, Peder, *From Bauhaus to Ecohouse: A History of Ecological Design* (Baton Rouge, LA: Louisiana State University Press, 2010).

Barker, Eileen, *New Religious Movements: A Practical Introduction* (London: HM Stationary Office, 1989).

Beevers, Robert, *The Garden City Utopia: A Critical Biography of Ebenezer Howard* (London: Macmillan, 1988).

Bellamy, Edward, *Looking Backward: 2007-1887* (Boston, MA: Ticknor and Company, 1888).

Bowen, Elizabeth, 'Notes on Writing a Novel', in *Collected Impressions* (New York: Alfred A Knopf, 1950).

Buder, Stanley, *Visionaries and Planners: The Garden City Movement and the Modern Community* (Oxford: Oxford University Press, 1990).

CABE (The Commission for Architecture and the Built Environment), *What it's like to live there: the views of residents on the design of new housing*, ed. Julian Birch (London: CABE, 2005).

Campbell, Beatrix, *Goliath: Britain's Dangerous Places* (London: Methuen, 1993).

Chase, Malcolm, *The People's Farm: English Radical Agrarianism 1775-1840* (London: Breviary Stuff Publications, 2010).

Coates, Chris, *Utopia Britannica: British Utopian Experiments, 1325 to 1945* (London: Diggers & Dreamers Publications, 2001).

Colls, Robert, *Identity of England* (Oxford: Oxford University Press, 2002).

Darley, Gillian, *Villages of Vision: A Study of Strange Utopias* (Nottingham: Five Leaves, 2007).

Darling, Elizabeth, *Re-Forming Britain: narratives of modernity before reconstruction* (London: Routledge, 2007).

Delaney, Miriam (ed.), *Utopia 7* (Dublin Institute of Technology, 2015).

Dorling, Danny, *All That is Solid: How the Great Housing Disaster Defines Our Times, and What We Can Do About It* (London: Allen Lane, 2014).

Ellis, Hugh, and Henderson, Kate, *Rebuilding Britain: Planning for a Better Future* (Bristol: Policy Press, 2014).

Evans, Dylan, *The Utopia Experiment* (London: Picador, 2015).

Fisher, Irving D, 'An Iconology of City Planning—The Plan of Chicago', in Erland Brock et al. (eds.), *Swedenborg and His Influence* (Bryn Athyn, PA: The Academy of the New Church, 1988), pp. 449-64.

Freudenheim, Leslie M, 'An Icon of Simplicity: The American Arts & Crafts Movement started at the Swedenborgian Church', at <http://www.shs.psr.edu/library/Freudenheim_article.asp>, accessed 4 June 2015.

Greenhalgh, Liz, *Habitat: Reconnecting Housing to City Policy* (London: Comedia/Demos, 1998).

Grindrod, John, *Concretopia: A Journey around the Rebuilding of Postwar Britain* (Brecon: Old Street, 2013).

Hall, Peter, and Ward, Colin, *Sociable Cities: The Legacy of Ebenezer Howard* (Chichester: John Wiley, 1998).

Hanley, Lynsey, *Estates: An Intimate History* (London: Granta Books, 2007).

Hardy, Dennis, *Alternative Communities in Nineteenth Century England* (London: Longman, 1979).

—— *Utopian England: Community Experiments 1900-1945* (London: E & FN Spon, 2000).

—— and Ward, Colin, *Arcadia for All: The Legacy of a Makeshift Landscape* (Nottingham: Five Leaves, 2004).

Hinchcliffe, Tanis, ' "The Synoptic View": Air Photographs and Twentieth-Century Planning', in *Camera Constructs: Photography, Architecture and the Modern City*, ed. Andrew Higgott and Timothy Wray (Aldershot: Ashgate, 2012).

Holliss, Frances, *Beyond Live/Work: The Architecture of Home-based Work* (Abingdon: Routledge, 2015).

Howard, Ebenezer, *Garden Cities of To-Morrow (being the second edition of 'To-morrow: A Peaceful Path to Real Reform')* (London: Swan Sonnenschein & Co., 1902).

Hunt, Tristram, *Building Jerusalem: The Rise and Fall of the Victorian City* (London: Weidenfeld and Nicholson, 2004).

Jackson, Frank, *Sir Raymond Unwin: Architect, Planner and Visionary* (London: Zwemmer, 1985).

Jellicoe, Geoffrey Alan, *Motopia: A Study in the Evolution of Urban Landscape* (London: Studio Books, 1961).

Jones, Tobias, *Utopian Dreams: A Search for a Better Life* (London: Faber, 2007).

Kynaston, David, *Austerity Britain 1948-51: Smoke in the Valley* (London: Bloomsbury, 2008).

— *Family Britain 1951-57* (London: Bloomsbury, 2009).

— *Modernity Britain: Opening the Box, 1957-59* (London: Bloomsbury, 2013).

Larkham, Peter J, and Lilley, Keith D, *Planning the 'City of Tomorrow': British Reconstruction Planning, 1939-1952—An Annotated Bibliography* (Pickering: Inch's Books, 2001).

Lebas, Elizabeth, *Forgotten Futures: British Municipal Cinema 1920-1980* (London: Black Dog Publishing, 2011).

Le Corbusier (pseud. Charles-Édouard Jeanneret-Gris), *Aircraft* (London: Trefoil Publications, 1987).

Linklater, Andro, *Owning the Earth: The Transforming History of Land Ownership* (London: Bloomsbury, 2014).

Lübbren, Nina, *Rural Artists' Colonies in Europe 1870-1910* (Manchester: Manchester University Press, 2001).

MacCarthy, Fiona, *The Simple Life: C.R. Ashbee in the Cotswolds* (London: Lund Humphries, 1988).

Mackail, J W, *The Life of William Morris*, 2 vols. (London: Longmans, Green & Co., 1899).

Markus, Thomas A, *Buildings and Power: Freedom and Control in the Origin of Modern Building Types* (London: Routledge, 1993).

Meek, James, 'Where will we live?', in *London Review of Books*, vol. 36, no. 1 (9 January 2014), pp. 7-16.

Méline, Jules, *Le retour à la terre et la surproduction industrielle* (Paris: Hachette et Cie., 1905).

Meller, Helen E, *Leisure and the Changing City 1870-1914* (London: Routledge & Kegan Paul, 1976).

—— *Towns, Plans and Society in Modern Britain* (Cambridge: Cambridge University Press, 1997).

Mill, John Stuart, *On Liberty* (London: John W Parker, 1859).

—— *Principles of Political Economy*, 2 vols. (London: John W Parker, 1848).

Morning Light: A New Church Weekly Journal (London: James Speirs, 1878-1914).

Morris, William, *News from Nowhere* (Boston, MA: Roberts Bros., 1890).

Municipal Dreams website, at <https://municipaldreams.wordpress.com>, accessed 29 July 2015.

Paine, Thomas, *Common Sense* (Philadelphia: R Bell, 1776).

Pinker, Susan, *The Village Effect: Why Face-to-Face Contact Matters* (London: Atlantic Books, 2015).

Power, Anne, and Tunstall, Rebecca, *Swimming Against the Tide: Polarisation or Progress on 20 Unpopular Council Estates, 1980-1995* (York: Joseph Rowntree Foundation, 1995).

Ravetz, Alison, *Council Housing and Culture: The History of a Social Experiment* (London: Routledge, 2001).

—— *The Government of Space: Town Planning in Modern Society* (London: Faber, 1986).

—— with Turkington, Richard, *The Place of Home: English Domestic Environments, 1914-2000* (London: E & FN Spon, 1995).

Richardson, Benjamin Ward, *Hygeia: A City of Health* (London: Macmillan and Co., 1876).

Saint, Andrew, ' "Spread the People": The LCC's Dispersal Policy, 1889-1965', in Andrew Saint (ed.), *Politics and the People of London: The London County Council, 1889-1965* (London: Hambledon Press, 1989).

Sennett, Richard, *Together: The Rituals, Pleasures and Politics of Cooperation* (London: Allen Lane, 2012).

Sharp, Thomas, *Town Planning* (Harmondsworth: Penguin, 1940).

Sutcliffe, Anthony, *Towards the Planned City: Germany, Britain, the United States and France, 1780-1914* (Oxford: Blackwell, 1981).

Swedenborg, Emanuel, *The New Jerusalem*, tr. John Chadwick (London: Swedenborg Society, 1990).

Tafuri, Manfredo, *The Sphere and the Labyrinth: Avant-Gardes and Architecture from Piranesi to the 1970s* (Cambridge, MA: MIT Press, 1992).

Thacker, Joy, *Whiteway Colony: The Social History of a Tolstoyan Community* (Stroud: Joy Thacker, 1993).

URBED (lead authors David Rudlin and Nicholas Falk), *Uxcester garden city: Second Stage Submission for the 2014 Wolfson Economics Prize* (Manchester: URBED, 2014).

Wallerstein, Immanuel, *Utopistics: Or, Historical Choices of the Twenty-First Century* (New York: The New Press, 1998).

Ward, Colin, *Anarchy in Action* (London: Freedom Press, 1982).

Washington, Peter, *Madame Blavatsky's Baboon: Theosophy and the Emergence of the Western Guru* (London: Secker & Warburg, 1993).

Webber, Melvin, 'The Urban Place and the Non-Place Urban Realm', in Melvin Webber (ed.), *Explorations into Urban Structures* (Philadelphia: University of Pennsylvania Press, 1964).

Weisman, Leslie Kanes, *Discrimination by Design: A Feminist Critique of the Man-Made Environment* (Chicago: University of Illinois Press, 1994).

Wilson, Elizabeth, *The Sphinx in the City: Urban Life, the Control of Disorder, and Women* (London: Virago Press, 1991).

Wordsworth, William, 'French Revolution, As it Appeared to Enthusiasts at its Commencement', in *Poems*, 2 vols. (London: Longman, Hurst, Rees, Orme, and Brown, 1815), vol. II.

Acknowledgements

I would like to thank Stephen McNeilly, James
Wilson and colleagues at the Swedenborg Society for
commissioning the lecture which gave rise to this essay,
and subsequently arranging for its publication. Thanks
also to Gareth Evans who effected the introduction and
provided other kindnesses along the way, as well as to
John Boughton of the website, *Municipal Dreams*,
and to Gillian Darley, Jason Orton, Andrew Saint and
Stephen Witherford. I am especially grateful to Liz
Greenhalgh who incisively commented on the first draft
of the text, and whose many pertinent comments and
questions have, I believe, resulted in a greatly improved
text. Finally, as always, I owe a great debt of thanks to
Larraine Worpole for her close editorial scrutiny, amongst
many other forms of encouragement and support.